MW01140347

Pandas

Victoria Blakemore

For Jen, the best pod-mate ever! I'd spare a square for you anytime.

vblakemore.author@gmail.com

Copyright info/picture credits

Cover, aloha2014/AdobeStock; Page 3, leungchopan/AdobeStock; Page 5, Robert Hainer/AdobeStock; Page 7, naraursu/AdobeStock; Page 9, Pexels/Pixabay; Pages 10-11, estivillml/AdobeStock; Page 13, Murd0k/Pixabay; Page 15, leungchopan/AdobeStock; Page 17, kennytong/AdobeStock; Page 19, wusuowei/AdobeStock; Page 21, silver-john/AdobeStock; Page 23; Pises Tungittipokai/AdobeStock; Page 25, Pexels/Pixabay; Page 27, aloha2014/AdobeStock; Page 29, aloha2014/AdobeStock; Page 31, wusuowei/AdobeStock; Page 33, StrangerView/AdobeStock

Table of Contents

What Are Pandas?

Pandas are large mammals known for their black and white coloring.

They have black patches on their eyes, ears, chest, and legs. The rest of their thick fur is white.

Panda fur is very thick and helps them to stay warm.

Size

Adult pandas are usually between four and five feet long. They may weigh up to 300 pounds.

Pandas are about the same size as an American black bear.

Male pandas are usually

larger than female pandas.

Physical Characteristics

No one is sure why pandas have their black and white fur. Some people think that it works as camouflage in the forest.

Pandas have large paws with claws that allow them to climb trees.

Pandas are very flexible, and are sometimes seen doing somersaults.

Habitat

Pandas live in the mountain forests of China. It is very wet and cool there, which is the kind of **climate** that pandas prefer.

The forests there are full of bamboo, which makes up most of a panda's diet.

Range

Pandas are only found in parts of southwestern China.

Pandas are usually very shy and prefer to stay away from places where humans are.

Diet

Pandas are **omnivores**, which means that they eat meat and plants.

Most of their diet is made up of bamboo, which they eat for up to sixteen hours every day.

Bamboo does not have many **nutrients**, so pandas may also eat small rodents, fish, birds, and insects.

Pandas have strong jaws and stomach muscles. This helps the pandas eat tough bamboo.

Pandas also have a special wrist bone that sticks out. They are able to use it like a thumb to grip bamboo as they are eating it.

Much of the water that

pandas get comes from the

bamboo that they eat.

Communication

Pandas sometimes communicate through sounds like bleats, honks, and growls. Much of their communication is through scent.

Pandas have a special scent gland that they use to mark their **territory**.

The scent may be used to

warn other pandas away or

help them find each other.

Movement

Pandas can run at speeds of up to 20 miles per hour when needed. They are not usually very active.

Between twelve and sixteen hours each day are spent eating bamboo.

Pandas are good climbers
and are often seen
perched on tree branches.

Solitary Life

Pandas are **solitary** animals, which means that they prefer to live alone.

Since pandas need to eat so much bamboo each day, they need a lot of forest space of their own. This makes sure that they have enough food.

Pandas have been **observed** living in small groups, but it is very rare.

Panda Cubs

Pandas have one or two babies, which are called cubs. When they are first born, cubs are very small, blind, and hairless.

Panda cubs are born in a den that the mother makes in a hollowed out log or tree stump.

Panda cubs stay with their mother for between one and three years.

Are Pandas Really Bears?

For many years, people were not sure if pandas were really bears. They were thought to be more closely related to raccoons.

Pandas were also thought to be related to red pandas, another Chinese mammal.

Scientists discovered that pandas are bears. They are not related to raccoons or red pandas.

Life Span

Not much is known about how long pandas live in the wild, but scientists think that it is around 20 years.

In zoos, pandas may live as long as 35 years.

Population

Pandas used to be **endangered**. Their populations have been growing, so they are now listed as **vulnerable**.

Studies estimate that there are between 1,600 and 1,900 pandas left in the wild.

There are more than 300 pandas living in zoos around the world.

Helping Pandas

People are trying to help the pandas in several ways.

Wildlife preserves have been set up around China. Bamboo forests are being protected and restored so that pandas have a safe habitat.

Some zoos train young pandas to survive in the wild.

The goal is to release more pandas into the wild so that panda populations can continue to grow.

Glossary

Climate: the usual weather in a place

Endangered: at risk of becoming extinct

Nutrients: things in food that help plants, animals, and people to grow

Observed: noticed or seen

Omnivore: an animal that eats meat and plants

Solitary: living alone

Territory: an area of land that an animal claims as its own

Vulnerable: an animal that is likely to become endangered

About the Author

Victoria Blakemore is a first grade teacher in Southwest Florida with a passion for reading.

You can visit her at

www.elementaryexplorers.com

Also in This Series

Also in This Series